Tudor Theatre

Katie Dicker

WAYLAND

...sion of
... Theatre
by Alan Childs

This edition first published in 2009 by Wayland

Copyright © Wayland 2009

Wayland
Hachette Children's Books
338 Euston Road
London NW1 3BH

Wayland Australia
Level 17/207 Kent Street
Sydney NSW 2000

Editor: Victoria Brooker
Designer: Simon Borrough

British Library Cataloguing in Publication Data:
  Dicker Katie
  Tudor theatre. - Differentiated ed. - (Be a history
  detective)
  1. Theatre - England - History - 16th century -
  Juvenile literature 2. Theatres - England - History -
  16th century - Juvenile literature England
  3. England - Social life and customs - 16th century -
  Juvenile literature
  I. Title II. Childs, Alan, 1942-
  792' .0942'09031

ISBN: 978 0 7502 5701 5

Printed and bound in China

Wayland is a division of Hachette Children's Books,
an Hachette UK Company.

www.hachettelivre.co.uk

Picture acknowledgements:
The publishers would like to thank the
following for permission to reproduce their
pictures: The Bridgeman Art Library 4, 7
(bottom-right), 8 (right), 12 (top), 16, 17
(bottom), 19 (top), 21 (bottom), 22 (bottom-
right); British Library 6; GGS Photographics
22 (candles etc.); Kippa Matthews 5; Mary
Evans Picture Library 15 (right), 21 (top);
Museum of London 12 (bottom), 27 (coin);
National Portrait Gallery 20 (top-left);
National Youth Music Theatre 11 (left) Kenn
Jacet, 11 (right) John Crook; Peter Newark's
Pictures cover and 7 (top), 10 (bottom-left),
25 (bottom), 26 (top-left), 29 (right); Ronald
Grant Archive 19 (bottom); Shakespeare's
Globe 1, 15 (top) Donald Cooper, 8 (left), 17
(top), 20 (bottom) John Tramper, 24 (both)
Richard Kalina, 27 (bottom) Tiffany Foster;
Theartarchive 28; Wayland Picture Library 9,
10 (right), 13, 14, 18, 22 (middle), 23, 29 (left).

Contents

Words in **bold** can be found in the glossary.

Theatre through the ages

Acting has been a popular activity for centuries. In Tudor times (1485–1603), people loved to act and to watch plays. Theatres began to develop into the type of entertainment we know today.

Religious plays

In the 13th century, many English towns began to put on religious plays. These were based on the lives of saints or stories from the Bible. Plays were performed in churches or on the streets. Some actors staged their plays on

The history detective, Sherlock Bones, will help you to find out more about Tudor theatre. Wherever you see one of Sherlock's paw-prints you

will find a mystery to solve. The answers can be found on pages 30 and 31.

▶ *This painting shows a stage put up in an old market square.*

wagons called pageants, which were pulled around the town. People either watched or acted – it was just like a modern carnival. In each town, there was a competition between workers to put on the best play. Sometimes, the workers chose Bible stories that matched their trade. The bakers might present the story of the Last Supper, for example, while the ship builders performed Noah's Ark.

From the play of 'Noah's Flood'.

Noah *Now in God's name I will begin*
To make the ship we shall go in,
When all the Earth,
through man's foul sin,
Shall lie beneath the flood.

[All, with the exception of Noah's wife, go through the motions of building the ark with various tools]

These boards I join together here
Shall bear [carry] us when the rains appear;
Then we shall sail both far and near
And safe be from the flood.

(Alexander Franklin, Seven Miracle Plays, OUP, 1963)

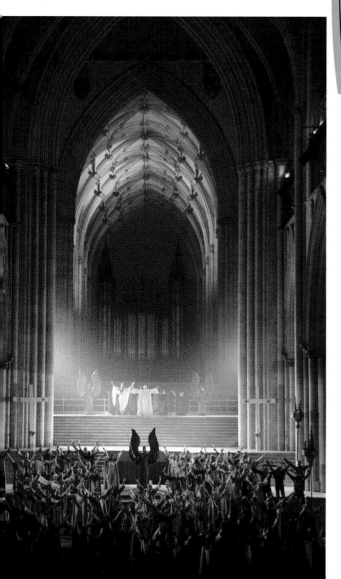

❧ Why do you think the bakers chose to perform the story of the Last Supper?

❧ Find out how the word 'pageant' is used today.

◄ *This photograph shows a modern religious play being performed in a cathedral.*

Detective work

Noye's Fludde is a musical written by Benjamin Britten. Ask your teacher to play a bit of it to your class. Can you hear the part where the animals go on to the ark?

Inn-yard theatres

In the summer, actors left the hot cities and travelled to the countryside. They set up their wagons in town squares where they performed plays to earn money. Actors began to realise that the local inns they were staying in made better theatres. The audience were nearby to pay when the collecting hat went round!

Entertainment at the inn

Actors built a stage in the inn's courtyard and the audience stood around. Guests staying at the inn could watch from the **galleries**. The audience paid to see the show when they arrived.

▼ *Queen Elizabeth I (1558–1603) liked to travel around the country in the summer months. Actors excaped the hot cities, too.*

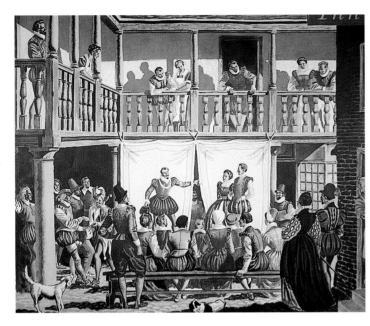

◄ *This simple stage has been set up at an inn. The audience are watching all around.*

❧ Which people in this inn-yard do you think had the best view of the play?

Full-time theatres

The audience could order food and drinks during the play. The innkeeper was pleased to have the extra trade. Soon, many inns were becoming full-time theatres. The standard of plays improved because the inns wanted to attract a bigger audience.

A famous Tudor actor called Edward Alleyn (1566–1626) often travelled around the country. He found ways to keep in touch with his wife while he was away:

I have sent you by this bearer, Thomas Pope's kinsman, my white waistcoat, because it is a trouble to me to carry it. Receive it with this letter, and lay it up for me till I come. If you send any more letters, send to me by the carriers of Shrewsbury or to West Chester...to be kept till my Lord Strange's Players come.

(Henslowe Papers, ed. Walter W Greg, 1907)

▼ *Inns served beer in big metal mugs called tankards.*

❧ How did Tudor actors such as Edward Alleyn send and receive their letters?

Acting work

In Tudor times, only boys and men could become actors. People did not think acting was a suitable job for women and girls. Boys dressed up in long skirts and wore face paints to play the female roles.

Detective work

Are there any acting companies in your area? Ask if they could talk to your class about their work. Do they perform any Tudor plays?

A licence to act

Tudor actors were treated very badly by the government. They were thought to be just like beggars. The government made a law insisting that acting groups had a **licence** to perform. They also had to be supported by a rich lord.

◄ *In Tudor times, boy actors dressed up to play the women's roles.*

Royal approval

Luckily, Queen Elizabeth I was kinder to actors. She and her **courtiers** loved to watch plays. For a time, there was a group of actors called *The Queen's Men*.

Earning a living

Actors in a **company** were paid wages. Young boys were taken on as **apprentices** to learn how to act. Theatre owners wanted their actors to stay for a long time so that their company would be a success.

Thomas Towne was an actor who got deeply into debt with his theatre owner, Philip Henslowe.

Sold unto Thomas Towne, player (actor),
a Black cloth cloak layed (covered) with silk lace
For xxvi^s viii^d to be payed by xii^d a week
and to begin payment the 2 of January 1597
and to continue weekly payment.
As lent unto Thomas Towne the 20 of March
1598 Ready money $\Big\}$ xii^d
Lent unto Thomas Towne (too) vpon a scarf. v^s

Henslowe's Diary, ed. Walter W Greg (1904)

Sometimes theatre owners lent money to their actors to buy expensive costumes. These loans would take months to pay back. Other actors had to promise to stay for a number of years before they were allowed to join a company.

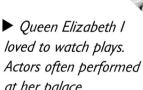

▶ *Queen Elizabeth I loved to watch plays. Actors often performed at her palace.*

🐾 How much, in shillings (s) and pence (d), was Thomas Towne's black cloak? How much was he going to pay Mr Henslowe each week?

🐾 Did Thomas Towne borrow any other money from Mr Henslowe?

Child actors

In Tudor times, children had few books at home or at school. They learnt their lessons by heart and acted out famous stories. During the holidays, some children performed plays for the public.

Choir schools

In London, some rich boys went to choir schools, such as St Paul's. They were given the chance to act in a children's drama group. Audiences paid to see them. It was hard work and sometimes the boys were treated cruelly. They had to go to lessons as well as lots of rehearsals.

▼ St Paul's Cathedral had a small playhouse used by the choir school boys.

▼ The boy actors performing at this wedding feast would have been very cold!

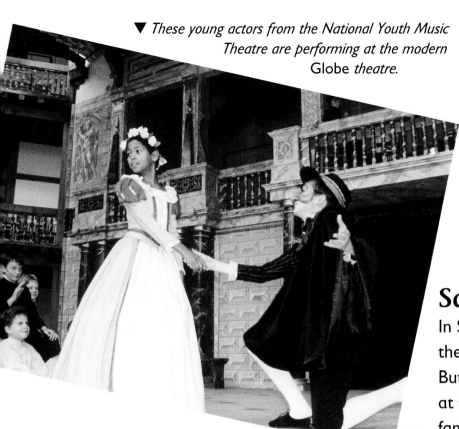

▼ These young actors from the National Youth Music Theatre are performing at the modern Globe *theatre*.

Salomon Pavey

In Shakespeare's play *Hamlet*, one of the characters teases the boy actors. But boy actors were often very good at their job. Salomon Pavey was a famous young actor who was brilliant at playing old men. He died when he was only 13 years old, probably from the **plague**.

'Twas a child that so did thrive
In grace and feature,
As Heaven and Nature seem'd to strive
Which owned the creature.
Years he numbered scarce thirteen
When Fates turn'd cruel,
Yet three filled Zodiacs had he been
The stage's jewel;
And did act (what now we moan)
Old men so duly
As sooth the Parcae (Fates) thought him one,
He played so truly.

(Ben Jonson, Epitaph for
Salomon Pavey, 1602)

Detective work

Try to find out about drama groups for young people in your area. What sort of plays do they perform?

❧ In the poem on the left Ben Jonson says that the 'Fates' killed 13-year-old Salomon Pavey by accident. Read the last four lines of this extract and work out why.

New Tudor theatres

In 1576, an actor called James Burbage built one of the first playhouses in London. It was called the *Theatre*. He built it north of London's city walls. He knew that if it was built in the city, the Lord Mayor might stop performances.

▼ *Philip Henslowe used to run bear-baiting contests. A chained bear was attacked by dogs while an audience watched.*

The *Rose* theatre

Burbage had a rival called Philip Henslowe. Henslowe wanted a brand-new theatre of his own. In 1587, he built the *Rose* theatre south of the River Thames in Southwark. This was another area outside the Lord Mayor's control.

Detective work

Find maps of Tudor London and look at the areas where theatres were built. Compare the maps with a map of modern London. How are they different?

Competition

When James Burbage died, his sons quarrelled with the landlord of the *Theatre*. They decided to pull the playhouse down and build a new theatre in Southwark called the *Globe*. When Henslowe found out, he ordered a larger theatre to be built at once, north of the city walls. He called it the *Fortune*.

▼ *The* Globe *and the* Rose *were built in Southwark, south of the River Thames.*

▲ *The original* Fortune *theatre burnt down in 1621. It was rebuilt in brick.*

❧ Why do you think Philip Henslowe wanted the *Fortune* theatre to be bigger than the *Globe*?

❧ Why would rebuilding a Tudor theatre be easier than rebuilding a modern building?

Philip Henslowe made a **contract** with his carpenter to build the *Fortune* theatre:

(The carpenter shall) provide and find all manner of workmen, timber, joists, rafters, boards, doors, bolts, hinges, brick, tile, lathe, lime, hair, sand, nails, lead, iron, glass, workmanship ... and shall also make all the said frame in every point for scantlings (dimensions) larger and bigger in assize (size) than the scantlings of the timber of the said new erected house called the Globe.

('Henslowe Papers', ed. Walter W Greg, Bullen, 1907)

Inside Tudor theatres

Tudor theatres were not very comfortable. There were only a few seats – most people stood up to watch the show. Many playhouses were open-air. If it rained, the audience got very wet!

▶ *This is a drawing of the* Swan *theatre (see page 15). It shows what the inside of a Tudor theatre looked like.*

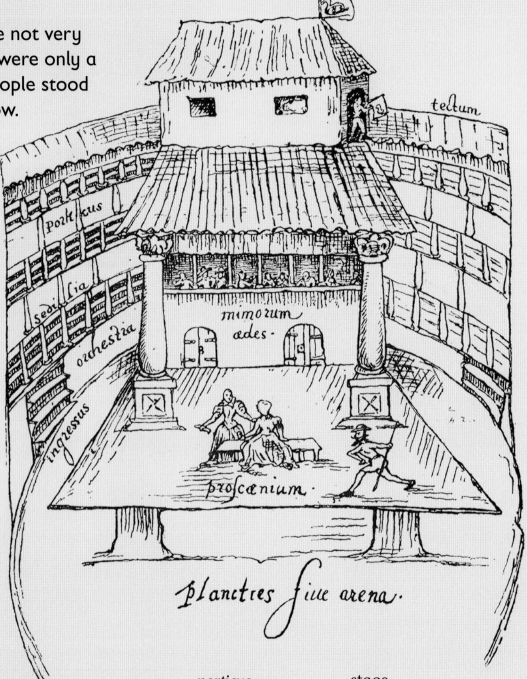

🐾 Look for these Latin words on the drawing of the *Swan* theatre. Can you match them with their English meanings?

porticus	stage
tectum	benches
mimorum aedes	seats for the wealthy
planities sive arena	roof
orchestra	actors' dressing room
ingressus	covered gallery
proscaenium	entrance to steps
sedilia	the yard

◀ *The modern* Globe *theatre presents plays in the style of Tudor times.*

Show time

The audience stood around the stage in the 'pit'. Rich spectators sat in the galleries above. During the performance, the audience were offered food and drink. The actors put on their costumes behind the stage. The **plot** was written on a piece of paper, pinned up by the door.

▲ *The audience was sometimes offered drinks during a play.*

In 1594, the *Swan* theatre was built in Southwark, not far from the *Rose*.

Of all the theatres, however, the largest and most distinguished is that wherof the sign is a swan ... since it has space for three thousand persons, and is built of a concrete of flint stones ... and supported by wooden columns, painted in such excellent imitation of marble that it might deceive even the most prying.

(Copy of letter by Johannes de Witt, c1596, University Library, Utrecht)

Stage scenery

There was a roof above the stage. The ceiling was often painted with pictures of stars and clouds. It was nicknamed the 'heavens'. A small curtained area at the back could be used to represent a cave or a bedroom. Above this, the balcony was useful to act out plays such as Shakespeare's *Romeo and Juliet*.

Special effects

There were plenty of surprises for Tudor audiences. In a sword fight, for example, an actor might appear to bleed red blood when the source of the cut was actually a hidden pig's bladder.

Secret doors

A wooden hut above the stage was often used to create special effects. A rope could be lowered through a trapdoor in the painted ceiling. A trapdoor on the stage could also leave audiences gasping.

There indeed a man may behold shaggy-haired devils run roaring over the stage with squibs in their mouths, while drummers make thunder in the tiring house, and the twelve penny hirelings make artificial lightning in their heavens.

(John Milton, 1620)

✤ What is another word for squibs? What were they used for?

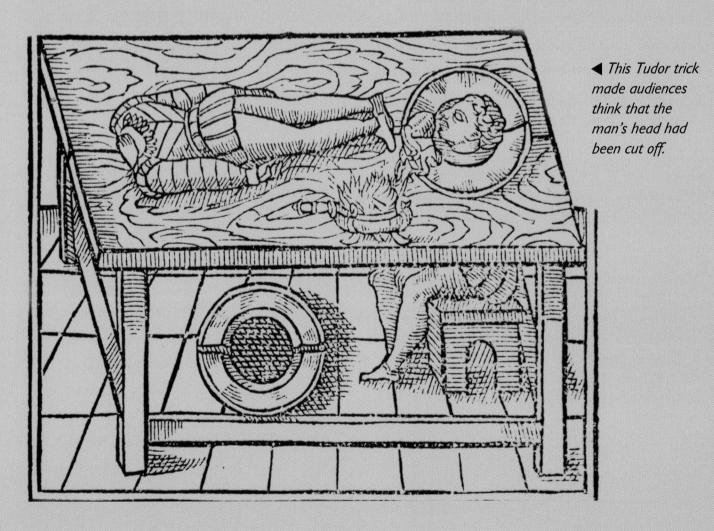

◀ *This Tudor trick made audiences think that the man's head had been cut off.*

▲ *A stage trapdoor is being used in this scene from Shakespeare's* Hamlet.

Detective work

Find out more about the use of special effects today. What modern special effects would have been impossible in Tudor times?

Sound effects

The Tudors loved lots of noise in their battle scenes. Sometimes, cannons were fired near to the theatre or small fireworks were set off by the stage. The sound of thunder was made by a drum, or by rolling real cannon balls around in a box.

▼ *This painting shows the beautiful scenery made for a Tudor play.*

Tudor audiences

If the theatre flag was flying, it meant that a performance would take place that day. At two o'clock, the trumpet blew and excited audiences hurried to the theatre. The show was about to begin!

▲ *These people are waiting to pay to go into a Tudor theatre.*

The audience

Almost every type of person went to the theatre – old and young, rich and poor. There were law students, market-women, shopkeepers and soldiers. Criminals went to the theatre, too. Plays were often noisy and while the audience watched the show, the **pickpockets** got up to their mischief.

Ticket prices

Just like today, theatres had different ticket prices. Poor people paid a penny to stand by the stage. Rich people paid more for a seat in the gallery. A cushion for the wooden benches cost another penny. The very rich might pay sixpence for a private room, or hire a stool to sit near the stage.

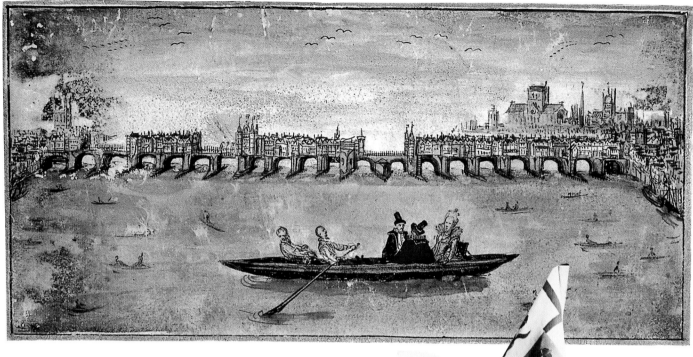

▲ *These boatmen are taking people across the River Thames to the theatre.*

Detective work

Ask your teacher if your class can watch the 1944 film of Shakespeare's *Henry V*. The first few scenes show views of Tudor London and a play at the *Globe*. What type of clothes are the audience wearing?

◄ *This famous actor, called Laurence Olivier, played the king in the 1944 film of Shakespeare's play* Henry V.

❀ Look at the picture above of the River Thames. What was unusual about London Bridge in Tudor times?

William Shakespeare

William Shakespeare was probably the world's most famous playwright. He was born in Stratford, England, in 1564 to a wealthy merchant and his wife. He decided to become an actor and then began to write plays himself.

The young actor

Shakespeare travelled to London to make his fortune. He joined the theatre group run by James Burbage's sons (see page 12). His first job was looking after the horses at the theatre. Then he began to take on small acting roles. When Shakespeare's gift for writing was discovered, he became a **sharer** in the company and helped to run it.

▲ *This portrait is believed to be of William Shakespeare.*

Detective work

Use books or the Internet to find out more about Shakespeare.

Are there any Shakespeare plays being performed in your area? When was the play written?

✿ Use books or the Internet to find out the name of the large house Shakespeare bought in Stratford.

✿ Shakespeare died on a special day of the year. What day was it?

◀ *Shakespeare's plays are still performed at the modern* Globe *theatre.*

▲ *This is the house in Stratford where Shakespeare was born.*

▼ *This painting shows Shakespeare with a group of friends, including the writer Ben Jonson, the poet John Donne and the adventurer, Sir Walter Raleigh.*

A successful career

Shakespeare wrote many of his plays for the *Globe* theatre. He knew what his audience liked and he wrote comic scenes that made them laugh. When Shakespeare finally returned to Stratford, he could afford one of the biggest houses in the town. He died on 23 April 1616.

Shakespeare's works

1590 *Henry VI, Part 1*
     Henry VI, Part 2
     Henry VI, part 3
1592 *Richard III*
     Titus Andronicus
1593 *The Comedy of Errors*
     The Taming of the Shrew
1594 *The Two Gentlemen of Verona*
     Love's Labour's Lost
1595 *Romeo and Juliet*
     Richard II
1596 *A Midsummer Night's Dream*
     King John
1597 *The Merchant of Venice*
     Henry IV, Part 1
1598 *Henry IV, Part 2*
     The Merry Wives of Windsor
1599 *Henry V*
     Much Ado About Nothing
     Julius Caesar
1600 *As You Like It*
     Twelfth Night
1601 *Hamlet*
1602 *Troilus and Cressida*
1603 *All's Well That Ends Well*
     Measure for Measure
1604 *Othello*
1605 *Timon of Athens*
1606 *King Lear*
     Macbeth
1607 *Antony and Cleopatra*
     Coriolanus
1608 *Pericles*
1609 *Cymbeline*
     (Sonnets published)
1610 *A Winter's Tale*
1611 *The Tempest*
1612 *Henry VIII*

Different types of theatres

Before Tudor times, plays were often performed in the great halls of large country houses. Wooden screens and balconies formed the stage. When the Tudors built theatres in London, however, they designed their buildings to be indoor or open-air.

Indoor theatres

Indoor theatres were much smaller than open-air theatres. There was no standing area and tickets were very expensive. Indoor theatres were useful in wintertime, or during bad weather. The Burbage theatre company used an indoor theatre as well as the open-air *Globe*.

◄ *Candles were used to light indoor theatres. The room could become very smoky.*

◄ *The first indoor theatres were the halls of large country houses.*

▼ *Travelling actors would entertain rich guests.*

Royal performances

Some actors were asked to perform their plays in front of Queen Elizabeth I. They would perform at palaces such as Whitehall. The companies would have to **audition**. No expense was spared for costumes or scenery.

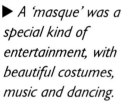

▶ A 'masque' was a special kind of entertainment, with beautiful costumes, music and dancing.

I saw the children of Paul's last night...
I' faith I like the audience that
  frequenteth there
With much applause: A man shall not be
  choked
With the stench of garlic, not be pasted
To the barmy jacket of a beer brewer...
'Tis a good gentle audience.
  (John Marston, Jack Drum's
    Entertainment, 1600)

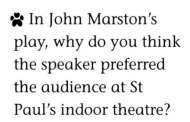

✿ In John Marston's play, why do you think the speaker preferred the audience at St Paul's indoor theatre?

Building Tudor theatres

▲ *The roof of the modern* Globe *was the first London building to be thatched in modern times.*

On a dark December night in 1598, a group of men joined Richard Burbage at the *Theatre*. They started to pull down the playhouse because of a quarrel with the landlord. The timbers were moved and rebuilt on the other side of the River Thames as the *Globe*.

Wooden framework

The framework of a Tudor building was made in a carpenter's yard before it was taken to the site. Oak wood was used which locked together as it dried and was fixed with wooden pegs. The foundations were made of crushed limestone and a brick wall was built for the wooden building to stand on.

▲ *In Shakespeare's original* Globe, *these beams would probably have been covered with plaster.*

🐾 Why did builders stop using thatched roofs in London after 1666?

Detective work

Are there any old Tudor houses in your area? Try to visit one, and look at how it was built. Look for the wooden pegs, the plaster and the small Tudor bricks.

Building materials

The framework was filled with strips of wood and covered with **plaster**, while the roof was thatched with reeds. Sand and crushed hazelnut shells were spread out on the floor to make a soft surface for the audience to stand on, and to absorb rainwater. Unfortunately, all these materials were a fire hazard. In 1613, the first *Globe* burnt down. Luckily, the 3,000 people in the audience managed to escape.

The King's Players had a new play (Henry VIII)... and certain cannons being shot off... some of the paper, or other stuff, wherewith one of them was stopped, did light on the thatch, where being thought at first but an idle smoke, and their eyes more attentive to the show, it kindled inwardly and ranround like a train (trail of gunpowder), consuming within less than an hour the whole house to the very ground.

(Henry Wotton – letter to Edmund Bacon, 1685)

▼ *When the second* Globe *was built in 1613 after the fire, the roof was made with tiles instead of thatch.*

❖ Why do you think the audience at the *Globe* did not notice that a fire had started?

Learning about the past

▼ *Archaeologists have to search through layers of buildings to uncover historic remains.*

By a stroke of luck, the old *Rose* theatre and the *Globe* were discovered in 1988–9, within a few months of each other. This was the first time that **archaeologists** could explore the remains of a Tudor theatre. The remains of the *Theatre* were also discovered in 2008.

Uncovering history

Archaeologists have to carefully remove layers of history that have been buried for hundreds of years. They found it easier to uncover the remains of the *Rose* theatre. The foundations of the *Globe* were buried underneath a main road and some houses. Both theatres had been taken down in the past, but their foundations revealed a lot of useful information.

Design details

At the *Globe*, for example, an outside stairway showed that rich people probably accessed the galleries from outside the theatre. At the *Rose*, the entrance door was very narrow. This narrow door

✤ Why is it difficult for archaeologists to work in a city such as London?

Detective work

Look at the *Globe's* website (http://www.shakespeares-globe.org/) and learn as much as you can about how this theatre was rebuilt in the 1990s. Ask if your teacher can arrange a class visit.

probably forced people to come through one at a time, to make sure that they paid money to see the show. Two sections of the original wall at the *Globe* also showed archaeologists what size and shape the original building was.

▶ *This coin was found in the remains of the* Rose *theatre.*

▼ *This photograph shows the modern* Globe *theatre being built.*

As archaeologists were pleading for more time to investigate the Elizabethan Rose Playhouse they believe they have found at Bankside, Southwark, South London, the... descendant of the man who built it, Mr Philip Henslowe, joined the campaign. Mr Henslowe... said: 'It is a key link with the theatre of our ancestors...' Mr C Walter Hodges, a theatre historian, said the find was the most important clue to Tudor entertainment since a drawing of the Swan Theatre... was found in 1888.

The Times, 15 February 1989

Your project

Topic Questions

1. How were Tudor theatres similar to inn-yard theatres?
2. Can you describe a year in the life of a Tudor actor?
3. What do we know about child actors in Tudor times?
4. Describe what it would have been like to visit a Tudor theatre.

Plan a project

1. Design a Tudor poster advertising a play. What information will the poster need? How will you encourage people to come to the play?

2. Imagine that you are a Tudor boy or girl visiting the *Globe*. Write a diary of your experiences.

3. Make a cut-away model of part of a Tudor open-air theatre, using the information in this book. You can use a large box to make the theatre and add a stage. You could use straws to make a 'thatch' roof and paint a gallery around the sides. Finally add peg-doll (or pipe-cleaner) figures for the actors and the audience.

4. Imagine that the Tudors could listen to the radio. Take your microphone to an imaginary 'Tudor theatre' and interview your classmates as the owner, the actors, or perhaps even William Shakespeare himself. What kind of questions would you ask?

5. Act out a short play about the night the old *Theatre* was taken down and moved across London Bridge to build the *Globe*.

▲ *When a Tudor actor called Will Kemp left Shakespeare's company he decided to dance from Norwich to London to attract attention.*

◀ *Richard Tarlton was Queen Elizabeth I's jester. He was one of the most famous Tudor comic actors.*

▶ *Shakespeare's friends made sure that his plays were published. Now future generations are enjoying them.*

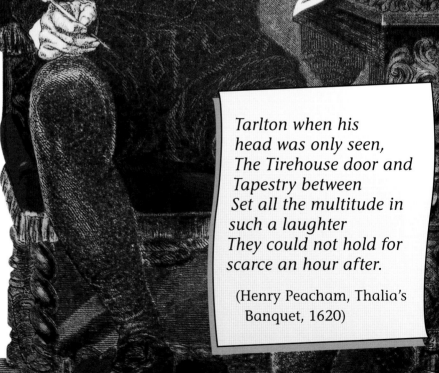

Richard Tarlton

A famous comic actor in Shakespeare's time, called Richard Tarlton, could make the audience laugh just by putting his head around the door. He also used a dog in his act. He wore country clothes and a cap and carried a pipe and a drum. When Tarlton died, his book of jokes was published.

Shakespeare based a character in one of his plays on Richard Tarlton. Can you find out who it is? Look up a play called *The Two Gentleman of Verona* (Act II, Scene III). What is the dog's name in the play, and his owner's name? Why is the owner annoyed with the dog?

Tarlton when his head was only seen, The Tirehouse door and Tapestry between Set all the multitude in such a laughter They could not hold for scarce an hour after.

(Henry Peacham, Thalia's Banquet, 1620)

Glossary

apprentice a young boy learning a trade.

archaeologist someone who studies the past by digging up remains.

audition a type of interview.

company a type of business.

contract a legal agreement between two people.

courtier a person who worked closely with the king or queen in Tudor times.

gallery a type of balcony that provides extra room for an audience.

licence a legal document allowing someone to own or do a particular thing.

pickpocket a thief who steals from someone's pockets.

plague a deadly disease in Tudor times.

plaster a substance used to cover walls or ceilings to form a smooth surface.

plot the main events in a play.

sharer a person who gives money to a company and earns money back if the company is successful.

Answers

☙ **page 5:** The Last Supper tells the story of Jesus sharing a meal of bread and wine with his disciples.

☙ Today, a 'pageant' can mean a grand performance or a procession. In Tudor times, plays were acted on pageant wagons. They were used in processions, too.

☙ **page 7:** The people in the front row probably had the best view. The people in the galleries had a higher viewpoint, but they were under cover if it rained!

☙ Letters would be sent by carriers' horses and carts, which travelled between towns.

☙ **page 9:** The cloak cost 26 shillings and 8 pence. The repayment was 12 pence a week.

☙ Thomas Towne also borrowed 'ready money' (12 pence) and a scarf (5 shillings).

☙ **page 11:** Ben Jonson is saying that Salomon was so good at playing the part of old men that the Fates caused him to die because they thought he was old.

☙ **page 13:** Philip Henslowe was an old rival of the Burbage family. In addition, he may have wanted his theatre to have more seats, to earn more money.

☙ It was easier to rebuild a Tudor theatre because it was made of wood. The sections could be taken apart and put back together again in a different place.

page 14:

porticus – covered gallery

tectum – roof

mimorum aedes – actors' dressing room

planities sive arena – the yard

orchestra – seats for the wealthy

ingressus – entrance to steps

proscaenium – stage

sedilia – benches.

page 16: Fireworks or explosives. They were used as sound effects.

page 19: There were houses built along London Bridge in Tudor times.

page 20: The house was called New Place.

Shakespeare died on St George's Day. St George is the patron saint of England.

page 23: He preferred the audience because they did not smell.

page 24: In 1666, parts of London were destroyed by a great fire. After this date, thatched roofs were not allowed in London.

page 25: The audience were concentrating on the play, or they might have thought the smoke was part of the special effects.

page 26: Over the centuries, many houses have been built in London, so layers of history have to be carefully removed.

Books to read

Tudor Theatre (Building History) by Gillian Clements (Franklin Watts, 2008)

Plays and the Theatre (Focus on Tudor Life) by Moira Butterfield (Franklin Watts, 2006)

The Timetraveller's Guide to Shakespeare's London by Joshua Doder (Watling St Ltd, 2004)

William Shakespeare: The Mystery of the World's Greatest Playwright by Rupert Christiansen (Short Books, 2004)

Shakespeare's London: A Guide to the Tudor City and Its Theatres by Julie Ferris (Kingfisher Books, 2000)

William Shakespeare and the Globe by Aliki (Mammoth, 2000)

William Shakespeare by Stewart Ross (Wayland, 2006)

Places to visit

Shakespeare's Globe
21 New Globe Walk,
Bankside, London SE1 9DT
The *Globe* also offers guided tours to the site of the *Rose* theatre, about 200 metres along bankside.
http://www.shakespeares-globe.org

Museum of London
150 London Wall,
London EC2Y 5HN
http://www.museumoflondon.org.uk

Index

Numbers in **bold** refer to pictures.